WHAT IS LOVE

DISCOVERING LOVE AND HATEFUL SENSATIONS

THE MIND BEHIND TEENAGE EYES

BRIAHNNA N. DOOLEY-NEWBILL

TABLE OF CONTENTS

Acknowledgements

To my parents, Cornell L. Newbill and Elizabeth A. Dooley, thank you for always supporting me in everything I do. You have given me my wings so that I can strive to reach my full potential. Thank you for loving me unconditionally.

To Katherine L. Dooley, thank you for inspiring me to pursue my writing goals. You have been with me every step of the way through the process of creating this work. None of this would be possible without you.

To Julian Creech, thank you for always seeing the best in my writing. You truly inspire me to continue doing what I love. You have seen the development of my writing over the past four years and have supported me every step of the way.

To Ariyan Shepherd, my number one supporter since day one. You always inspire me to be myself and express myself in every way possible. These words of self expression would not be on these pages without you.

To all of my family and friends, thank you for the never ending love and support.

Thank you to my readers. Your support is everything.

Preface

My collection "What is Love" encompasses many complex relationships. Some of which are, emotional connectivity, power and authority, and society and the individual. "Discovering Love" is written from my perspective based on the deepening emotion that comes with exploring feelings and discovering the end of something you thought was meant to be perfect but in fact it was flawed.

"Hateful Sensations" is written from my perspective on the power of love and the notion that love changes people. The inspiration to write this collection came from many recent events of 2020 and the injustice minorities have faced in America for many years. Love is a binding force that can be used to create greater change for the future.

Without love there is no change or growth. In this two part collection, I use the power of words to express my experiences as a teenager transitioning into young adulthood. We must work through changes by learning to love and grow.

Briahnna D-N.
June 8, 2020

DISCOVERING LOVE

ONE

ONE

it all started with a pencil
the day she met her love
she thought it couldn't possibly be him, he isn't the one

big mind
big heart
warm smile

the way his words left his lips
oh so swift
like he had done this all before

big mind
big heart
warm smile

five words
she looked up
seven words
she smiled
five more
their hearts intertwined

. . . .

WANTING TO GIVE HER THE WORLD

i'd love you for eternity
if you'd let me
dreams of what could be

take me by the hand
only you understand the way I breathe
sentiment

F

FALLING...3

he was the sun on her rainy days
her smile when she couldn't hide the pain

the one she stayed up and talked to
someone once said, "i don't care if I lose sleep talking to him"
that's how she felt about him

I

FALLING...2

life is like music
you are my song
stuck on repeat in my head

mind flooded with thoughts of you
feelings that I cannot express to you
because of the way I feel for you

life is like music
you are my song
with an endless melody
you keep me singing

you are my song
stuck in my head
every word you said
on repeat in my head

an endless melody
what I hope we could be
a never ending memory

V

. . . .

FALLING...1

she loved him from the start
hoping they would never part
maybe in space but never at heart

E

HE

he was just a boy
a boy with a big heart
afraid to show people what he really feels
because he doesn't know how to deal with the pain
his life is an endless chase

running from the thoughts that could consume him
he's afraid that he'll lose himself if he lets them in
he keeps running

running until finally all that's left is a trail of broken pieces
people he's left behind
people who loved him

he didn't let them in because he was afraid of what love could do
he believed you shouldn't let it consume you because of the pain it
could bring
and that's all he ever knew

S

SHE

she was a girl
a girl with a big heart
she saw beauty in his eyes
comfort in his smile

she wanted to love him
but not in this way
this way can consume you

E

. . . .

THINKING ABOUT YOU

never knew what a hug could
do
never knew the impact you
had
never knew I was actually sad
seldom did you even bother
to
ask
what a simple task
never should have bought
into
you
oh, the things you do

thought we would be stuck
like
glue
started something new
then you came and changed
the rules
what a selfish thing to do

he was just a kid
we never knew he was
hurting
because of the things they
did
to you
never knew the impact they
had
never knew they made a
young
boy sad
what a bad way to love
someone

now he will never know how
to love
without bringing someone
else down
letting people in
leaving them wondering what
could have been
should have never let them in

never does she know how to
feel
little does he know how to
heal
having each other, that was
real

V

WITHOUT YOU

nothing feels right without you
-your love

UNFORGETTABLE

their love for each other was like something out of a movie
so sudden yet still
unforgettable
impossibly erasable

i still care for you
i think about you everyday
this was all she wanted to say

. . . .

CHANGES

i'll never forget the moment when I began to hope you'd stay
forever
but we just weren't meant to be together
thought we'd stay together no matter the weather
but our love, it began to feather
i wonder if you even cared for me
whether you dreamed of what could be
but just maybe we weren't meant to be

if the good outweighs the bad keep him in your life

MISSING YOU

i miss your kiss more than
anything right
now
i wish I could feel your lips
against mine
one more time
i miss you but not us

i'm missing you
i miss kissing you
when I was with you
all I wanted was to love you
-she

it's over now
all that's left are these empty
thoughts
empty feelings

i no longer feel you
i just want to keep things real
with you

but I still miss kissing you
-he

she doesn't love you
not the way I would have
loved
you
-she

incomplete but we complete
each other
not the way the earth needs
the
sun
we don't need each other like
they do
we aren't meant to be
together
you just miss kissing me

the last time I kissed you
well I don't remember
but that was a time when we
didn't think
we would last
i guess we were right
-them

I

. . . .

TIRED

it's you
always you
no matter what I do
i still think about you

used to always see the good in you
now all I want is to hate you
so sick of loving you

broken now
just hoping now
for another chance
not a chance with you
someone who cares more than you

V

. . . .

EMPTY

there was a time when you wanted me
but now it seems you only wanted the pieces of me

i used to think of all the things we could be
dreams about you and me
even after everything you said
i thought maybe we could be happy
but there is no more we
so how could we ever be happy

should have trusted my gut
i saw all the things you were, before you spoke those 5 little words

OUT OF SIGHT OUT OF MIND

out of sight, out of mind
they say out of sight, out of mind
you're out of sight but you're still on my mind

out of sight, out of mind
but everything that has happened between us, is still on my mind

out of sight, out of mind
i want to keep my distance but I can't let you go

out of sight, out of mind
still remembering you but trying to hide the pain

out of sight, out of mind
they say out of sight ,out of mind
but your always on my mind

L

. . . .

MEMORIES OF YOU

songs in my head remind me of you
bringing back memories of me and you

0

. . . .

ONE UNFORGETTABLE MOMENT

only for a moment
i just want one moment
an unforgettable moment with you

only for a moment
the world will stop
it's just you and me
just in that moment
a moment with you

the time will pass
it won't last
but i'll never forget
this moment with you

V

YOU'RE BIGGER

you're bigger than broken promises
bigger than the shit that he gave you
the pain does not define you
what defines you is how you deal with the pain
do you grow or let it consume you?

SENTIMENT

sentiment but not sentimental
you can choose to love me
but I'm not a rental

take my heart

i loved you from the start
but you don't deserve this piece of my heart
i am a work of art

WHAT IS LOVE?

what is love
a four letter word
but what is the meaning

"love is just love it's not always perfect"

IS IT WORTH THE PAIN?

loving someone who no longer wants your love
all along you cared
cared so much you began to love
but sometimes you have to let go
other times you have to know when to hold on
when to hold on to the ones that are worth it
when to hold on to the feeling of love that mean more than the
pieces
it left behind

sometimes holding on is harder than letting go
other times letting go is worse than holding on
they say that time heals
they say that you will be okay
but if you just let time go by and let go of what you loved are you
healing
or forgetting the feeling
the feeling you felt when you loved someone who was really worth
it

A LOVE LETTER TO YOU

love, a four letter word that can mean more than anything you've
ever
heard
i believe love in itself is something we share
the kind of love you feel when you know someone cares

love runs deeper than oceans
love changes people
love is how we grow

HATEFUL SENSATIONS

INSIGHT

"THIS IS A TIME FOR AMERICA TO LOOK AT HOW THEY LOOK AT MINORITIES. EITHER YOU LIVE OR YOU DIE BY YOUR STEREOTYPES. EITHER YOU LIVE OR YOU DIE BY YOUR IGNORANCE, YOU KNOW? EITHER WE CHANGE OR WE ALL FALL"
-TUPAC, 1992

A LETTER TO LOVE

DEAR LOVE,
WE NEED YOU NOW
FILL OUR HEARTS AND MINDS
FOR YOU CAN DROWN OUT HATE

NOTHING IS EVER DESTROYED COMPLETELY
BUT WITH YOU WE CAN MAKE A BIG CHANGE

DEAR, LOVE
PLEASE SHOW UP
OPEN OUR MINDS
YOU GIVE US HOPE FOR THE FUTURE

ANGER IS A MASK

THEY SAY HATE IS A STRONG WORD
BUT SOMETIMES OTHER WORDS HIT MUCH HARDER
I'D RATHER SOMEONE TELL ME STRAIGHT
RIGHT TO MY FACE
THAN TO KEEP TREATING ME BADLY
WHEN WE REALLY LOVE EACH OTHER MADLY
HOW COULD WE POSSIBLY HATE

ALWAYS CRY
NEVER SAY GOODBYE
DON'T KNOW HARD TIMES BUT I CONSIDER THESE MINE
A WAR AGAINST HATE
HOPE IT ISN'T FATE
THEY SAY JUST WAIT
TIME WILL HEAL BUT THEY DON'T KNOW WHAT I REALLY FEEL

I AM A BLACK GIRL IN AMERICA

I AM A BLACK GIRL IN AMERICA
EDUCATED, BEAUTIFUL AND STRONG
BUT WHY IS IT WHEN YOU SEE MY BROTHER JUST THE SAME AS ME YOU FEEL
THREATENED

I AM A BLACK GIRL IN AMERICA
I AM BLESSED AND PRIVILEGED
BUT MY SKIN DOES NOT PROVIDE ME WITH THAT PRIVILEGE

I AM A BLACK GIRL IN AMERICA
I HAVE DONE NOTHING WRONG
I WANT PEACE AS MUCH AS YOU
BUT WHY IS IT WHEN YOU SEE MY BROTHER JUST THE SAME AS ME YOU FEEL
THREATENED.

I AM A BLACK GIRL IN AMERICA
PROFILED, STEREOTYPED
BUT THIS DOES NOT DEFINE ME

FOR I AM A BLACK GIRL IN AMERICA
EDUCATED, BEAUTIFUL AND STRONG
YOUR HATE WILL NEVER DEFINE ME

THE EYES OF RACIST AMERICA

Our silence angers them but so do our voices
Kneeling peacefully, they are offended
And oh, speaking up is far too much
In the eyes of racist America

We are demanding equality not superiority
Why is it so hard for you to see
we want justice not "just us"
How do you not see
We all just want to be free

Threatened but not a threat

Weight of the world on our shoulders
Looking at us sideways
As if we are the problem

Minding my business
They don't mind theirs
But still, I am the problem
In the eyes of racist America

WHEN TWO PATHS COLLIDE

WHEN TWO PATHS COLLIDE
IT COULD BE BITTER OR SWEET
AT FIRST IT SEEMS YOU MUST ABIDE BY SIMPLE RULES

WHEN TWO PATHS COLLIDE
YOU SIMPLY WANT TO PASS BY JUST GLIDE
BUT REMEMBER ITS A COLLISION
VERY LITTLE TIME FOR DECISION
WHEN TWO PATHS COLLIDE

FIRE

THEY SAY HISTORY REPEATS ITSELF BUT WHEN DOES THIS END
WHAT IS THE POINT OF PROGRESSION IF YOU DO NOT LEARN A LESSON
YOU CANNOT SEE THE BIGGER PICTURE
HATE ONLY DESTROYS
IT DOES NOT MAKE YOU STRONGER

DECADES

DECADES OF DEATH
DECADES OF HATE
HOW MANY TIMES DO WE HAVE TO FALL
BEFORE THERE IS NOTHING LEFT BUT BURNING HATE

THIS IS NOT A WAR BETWEEN LOVE AND HATE THIS IS A WAR AGAINST HATE
DEEPENING WOUNDS
BUT STILL WE WILL RISE AND TRY TO HEAL

FEELING

LIKE

I'M

ALWAYS

 IN

MY

HEAD

 LOOKING

FROM

THE

OUTSIDE.

MORE LOVE

HOW CAN WE GIVE SO MUCH HATE
BUT SO LITTLE LOVE
HATE AND LOVE TWO FOUR LETTER
WORDS THAT CAN CHANGE THE
WORLD

CHANGE
WE HAVE TO BE THE ONES TO MAKE
CHANGE
WE HAVE TO COME TOGETHER
DESPITE OUR DIFFERENCES
DESPITE THE HATE
DESPITE THE BONDAGE YOU MAY FEEL

OUR STRUGGLES MANY BE DIFFERENT
WE ALL COME FROM DIFFERENT
WALKS OF LIFE
BUT WE ARE ALL ONE RACE THE
HUMAN RACE
ALL WONDERFULLY AND BEAUTIFULLY
MADE
ALL SPECIFICALLY DESIGNED TO
FOLLOW THE PATH OF LIFE
WE ALL WANT TO REACH GOALS
SO WHO ARE YOU TO JUDGE
SOMEONE BECAUSE OF THE WAY THEY
SPOKE TO YOU

BECAUSE OF THE WAY THEY LOOKED
AT YOU
JUDGEMENT IS OFTEN A POOR
PERCEPTION
WE PLACE JUDGEMENT ON PEOPLE
BECAUSE SOCIETY TELLS THEY ARE
DIFFERENT
BUT AREN'T WE ALL DIFFERENT
WE ARE DIFFERENT BUT WE ALL HAVE
A PURPOSE
WE SHOULD NOT JUDGE PEOPLE
BASED ON THE COLOR OF THEIR SKIN
OR THE LANGUAGE THEY SPEAK
THE WAY THEY SPOKE TO YOU
THE WAY THEY LOOKED AT YOU

CHANGE WILL TAKE TIME BUT WITH
THIS IN MIND
I HOPE YOU'LL TAKE TIME TO SPREAD
LOVE AND NO MORE HATE
WHAT GOOD DOES HATE EVER DO
AND I DON'T KNOW ABOUT YOU
BUT I'VE SEEN WHAT LOVE CAN DO
SO SPREAD YOUR LOVE ALL AROUND
SHOW PEOPLE THAT YOU CARE
AND TOGETHER WE CAN SPREAD
MORE LOVE AND LESS HATE

TEACH THEM TO LOVE

TEACH THEM TO LOVE SO THAT OUR CHILDREN CAN STAND TOGETHER WITH
PRIDE RATHER THAN FEAR
TEACH THEM SO THAT THEIR FUTURE CAN BE BRIGHT NO MATTER THE COLOR OF
THEIR SKIN

TEACH THEM
BRING JUSTICE AND EQUALITY TO LIFE
WE PREACH THESE WORDS OVER AND OVER
LITTLE BY LITTLE WE PUSH FORWARD
DESPITE THE HATE

WE CANNOT BREAK
FOR OUR GENERATION IS THE NEXT FORMATION OF THE HUMAN RACE
LOVE WILL BIND US
TOGETHER WE CAN DROWN OUT THE HATE

About the Author

Briahnna Dooley-Newbill is a
multitalented, 2020 high
honors high school graduate.
Briahnna will attend college in
the fall pursuing a major in
psychology with the ultimate
plan to pursue a Ph.D in
psychology. She will continue
her writing along with pursing
professional goals that allows
her to be a guiding hand to
those in need, and also help

them achieve both personal and large scale change. Briahnna has
experienced first hand, how even the best laid plans may often change.
While her future evolves and her life continues to change, she will
forever seek to pursue excellence.

In the midst of COVID 19 and social injustices the author's creative
mind and spirit allow her to use a form of realism, personal
experiences, and everyday situations to construct her poetry. During
times of uncertainty the author chose to unleash her creative talents
that allowed her to create a body of work that amplifies the voice of a
young adult.